Three Decades

to Rescue The Earth

Wu Jui Pao

In Taiwan

http://coco00.webnode.tw

http://20140129.blogspot.com

http://tomu18.webnode.tw

http://20140214.blogspot.com

ISBN:1514301822
ISBN-13: 978-1514301821

DEDICATION

Thanks my wife, who depend on me to write many books.
She is also an author in Taiwan, and edited our books.

CONTENTS

Three decades to rescue the Earth

I have a dream, keeping the world safe avoid hurt from pesticides and chemical fertilizers, and I have confirmed that there are ways.

The first ten years, I used the symbiosis of nature agriculture and forest farm, have practical experience, and are producing good fruit and vegetables for me and others to eat.

In the process of planting, I used the symbiotic concept of agriculture, no chemical fertilizers, no weed killer herbicides and no pesticides, using only natural plant weeds, tea leaves, bean residue, chaff, and all crops at harvest time, broken branches, let it decomposed after fermentation, become fertilizer, in this way, plant crops, grow very healthy nutrition.

At the same time I wrote the agriculture books of "Pingtung Boy Tom" and "Symbiosis of Agriculture" with cost books, and authored the "Symbiosis of Agriculture and Forest cultivation" of illustrated book for free, for everyone to read and share this success experience with all.

Now entering its second decade, I would like to invite 10,000 people, their farming community in the fields, to participate in the revolutionary ideal of symbiosis of agriculture forest farming.

Each one has 30 to 50 square meters of land, arable use.

At present Taiwan rent of agricultural land in the South, point zero one acre about 5,000 yuan. Take into account the large area, if each person 50 ping, ten person 500 pings ... 10,000 people 500,000 square feet, about 160 a few hectares, the much more pings with lower rents.

About 160 a few hectares around, planting full of trees, each one allocate 20 ping of land to create a forest green.

And then their self-assigned to land, 30 ping land can grow three to six variety of vegetables, fruit trees, three ping took shelter species of sponge gourd, pumpkin, family consumption throughout the year, as long as you work hard enough, it must have been enough.

Finally third decade and I want to expand that success experience, from about 160 to 1600 hectares ... Until hundred, thousand, million and million hectares, even the concept of forest cultivation can be used all over the world, to save the Earth from disaster.

.

1 CHAPTER:2009

PICTURE 1-1

PICTURE 1-2

PICTURE 1-3

PICTURE 1-4

PICTURE 1-5

2 CHAPTER:2010

PICTURE 2-1

PICTURE 2-2

PICTURE 2-3

PICTURE 2-4

PICTURE 2-5

3 CHAPTER:2011

PICTURE 3-1

PICTURE 3-2

PICTURE 3-3

PICTURE 3-4

PICTURE 3-5

4 CHAPTER:2012

PICTURE 4-1

PICTURE 4-2

PICTURE 4-3

PICTURE 4-4

PICTURE 4-5

5 CHAPTER:2013

PICTURE 5-1

PICTURE 5-2

PICTURE 5-3

PICTURE 5-4

PICTURE 5-5

6 CHAPTER:2014

PICTURE 6-1

PICTURE 6-2

PICTURE 6-3

PICTURE 6-4

PICTURE 6-5

PICTURE 6-6

PICTURE 6-7

PICTURE 6-8

PICTURE 6-9

7 CHAPTER:2015

PICTURE 7-1

PICTURE 7-2

PICTURE 7-3

PICTURE 7-4

PICTURE 7-5

PICTURE 7-6

PICTURE 7-7

PICTURE 7-8

PICTURE 7-9

PICTURE 7-10

PICTURE 7-11

8 CHAPTER:FOREST

PICTURE 8-1

PICTURE 8-2

PICTURE 8-3

PICTURE 8-4

PICTURE 8-5

PICTURE 8-6

PICTURE 8-7

PICTURE 8-8

PICTURE 8-9

PICTURE 8-10

PICTURE 8-11

PICTURE 8-12

ABOUT THE AUTHOR

Wu Jui Pao loves swimming, flying, playing tennis, bicycling, horseback riding, traveling many countries and meeting people.
He lives very colorfully, so that want to write the books telling others.
"Pingtung Boy Tom" is about his childhood rural farmers life.
"Three Decades to Rescue The Earth" and "Symbiosis Agriculture" is his dreams.
Now he and his wife enjoy themselves farming and writing.

www.ingramcontent.com/pod-product-compliance
Lightning Source LLC
Chambersburg PA
CBHW050810290526
45792CB00001B/53